From Nothing to Something New

Insights on Startups and Building the Future Through Innovation.

Jorge Watson

COPYRIGHT MESSAGE

All rights reserved. No part of this publication may be reproduced, distributed, or transmitted in any form or by any means, including photocopying, recording, or other electronic or mechanical methods, without the prior written permission of the publisher, except in the case of brief quotations embodied in critical reviews and certain other noncommercial uses permitted by copyright law.

Copyright © Jorge Watson (2024)

Table of Contents

Introduction
- A brief overview of innovation and the significance of developing original ideas.

Chapter 1. **Vertical Progress vs. Horizontal Progress**
- An explanation of the difference between inventing new concepts and expanding existing ones.

Chapter 2. **Monopoly vs. Competition**
- The benefits of having a monopoly and the drawbacks associated with competition.

Chapter 3. The **Power of Technology**
- An exploration of how technology drives advancement and fosters innovation.

Chapter 4. **The Importance of a Strong Founding Team**
- The critical role of a unified team in overcoming obstacles.

Chapter 5. **Sales and Distribution Matter**
- The importance of effective sales techniques in conjunction with product development.

Chapter 6. **The Future of Startups**
- Perspectives on how innovative startups will influence future developments.

Chapter 7. **Contrarian Thinking**
- The significance of challenging conventional beliefs to discover unique opportunities.

Chapter 8. **The Role of Secrets**
- The value of undiscovered insights that lead to successful startups.

Chapter 9. **Long-Term Planning**
- Advantages of prioritizing sustainable growth rather than focusing solely on immediate results.

Chapter 10. **The Importance of Culture**
- How a robust company culture encourages innovation and teamwork.

Conclusion
- A call to action for entrepreneurs to chase original ideas and contribute to future innovations.

Introduction

In an era characterized by rapid technological advancements and ever-evolving consumer demands, the concept of innovation has emerged as a cornerstone for success in the business landscape. The phrase "from nothing to something new" encapsulates the essence of startups, which often begin as mere ideas and transform into groundbreaking enterprises that reshape industries. At the heart of this transformation lies innovation—a powerful force that not only drives economic growth but also fosters creativity and addresses pressing societal challenges.

Innovation is more than just a buzzword; it represents a mindset that values curiosity, experimentation, and a willingness to explore uncharted territories. It is the process of turning original ideas into tangible products or services that create value for consumers. In today's competitive market, where established players can quickly become obsolete, startups that harness the power of innovation are better positioned to disrupt traditional paradigms and capture market share.

The Importance of Innovation

The importance of innovation cannot be overstated. It serves as a catalyst for economic development, job creation, and enhanced quality of life. Innovative companies are often at the forefront of their industries, leading the charge in technological advancements and setting trends that others strive to follow. For instance, companies like Apple and Tesla have not only revolutionized their respective markets but have also inspired countless entrepreneurs to think differently and pursue their visions.

Moreover, innovation fuels competition, which ultimately benefits consumers. As startups introduce new products and services, established companies are compelled to adapt and improve their offerings. This dynamic creates a vibrant marketplace where consumers have access to a diverse range of choices, driving down prices and enhancing quality. In this context, innovation becomes a key driver of progress, pushing boundaries and challenging the status quo.

The Significance of Developing Original Ideas

At the core of successful innovation lies the development of original ideas. Originality is what differentiates a startup from its competitors; it is the unique perspective that enables entrepreneurs to identify gaps in the market and create solutions that resonate with consumers. When startups prioritize originality, they not only carve out a niche for themselves but also contribute to the overall advancement of their industries.

The significance of original ideas extends beyond mere differentiation; it also fosters a culture of creativity and exploration. When entrepreneurs" mindset embrace originality, they encourage their teams to think outside the box, experiment with new concepts, and challenge conventional wisdom. This culture of innovation cultivates an environment where creativity flourishes, leading to breakthroughs that can have far-reaching implications.

Furthermore, original ideas are crucial for addressing complex societal challenges. In a world facing issues such as climate change, healthcare disparities, and social inequality, innovative solutions are essential for driving positive change. Startups that focus on developing original ideas can create products and services that not only meet consumer needs but also contribute to the greater good. For instance, companies working on renewable energy technologies or affordable healthcare solutions are examples of how innovation can lead to meaningful societal impact.

Creating Something New Versus Copying

While the allure of copying successful models may seem tempting, it often leads to stagnation and missed opportunities. Imitation may provide short-term gains, but it lacks the transformative power of originality. Startups that rely on copying existing ideas risk blending into a sea of sameness, unable to establish their unique identity or value proposition.

The dangers of copying extend beyond mere market positioning; they also stifle creativity within organizations. When teams perceive that imitation is rewarded over innovation, they become less inclined to propose original ideas. This creates a culture of complacency where mediocrity prevails, ultimately hindering growth and progress. On the other hand, fostering an environment that celebrates originality encourages risk-taking and experimentation—key ingredients for innovation.

Moreover, in an age where consumers are increasingly discerning, authenticity matters more than ever. Today's consumers seek brands that resonate with their values and offer unique experiences. Startups that prioritize creating something new stand a better chance of building strong relationships with their customers. By offering original products or services that reflect their vision and mission, these startups can cultivate brand loyalty and differentiate themselves in a crowded marketplace.

Conclusion

The journey from nothing to something new is emblematic of the startup experience—one filled with challenges, opportunities, and endless possibilities. At the heart of this journey is innovation, a powerful force that drives economic growth and societal advancement. By prioritizing original ideas and embracing creativity, startups can carve out their unique identities and create meaningful solutions that address real-world problems.

As we look toward the future, it is essential for entrepreneurs to recognize the significance of developing something new rather than resorting to imitation. In doing so, they not only contribute to their own success but also play a vital role in shaping a more innovative and dynamic business landscape. The future belongs to those who dare to dream big, think differently, and transform their visions into reality—turning nothing into something new.

Chapter 1

Vertical Progress vs. Horizontal Progress

In the dynamic world of innovation and entrepreneurship, understanding the distinction between vertical and horizontal progress is crucial for aspiring creators and business leaders. These two concepts represent different approaches to growth and development, each with its unique implications for discovering lucrative ideas. While both paths can lead to success, they require distinct mindsets, strategies, and methodologies.

Defining Vertical Progress

Vertical progress refers to the advancement that occurs through the invention of new concepts, technologies, or methodologies. It embodies a transformative approach where ideas are not merely expanded upon but are entirely reimagined. This type of progress is characterized by breakthroughs that disrupt existing markets or create entirely new ones. Think of vertical progress as climbing a mountain; each step upward represents a significant leap in understanding or capability that has the potential to redefine an industry.

For instance, consider the development of smartphones. Before their introduction, mobile phones were primarily used for calls and texts. The invention of the smartphone transformed this concept into a multifunctional device that combined communication, computing, and entertainment in one portable gadget. This vertical leap not only created a new market but also revolutionized how people interact with technology daily.

Vertical progress often involves significant research and development (R&D) investments, as it requires a deep understanding of existing technologies and consumer needs. Innovators engaged in vertical progress are typically motivated by a desire to solve complex problems or fulfill unmet needs in novel ways. This process can be risky, as it demands substantial resources and may not always lead to immediate financial returns. However, when successful, vertical innovations can yield high rewards and establish a lasting legacy.

Understanding Horizontal Progress

In contrast, horizontal progress involves expanding upon existing concepts, products, or services rather than inventing entirely new ones. This approach focuses on refinement, enhancement, and diversification. Horizontal progress can be likened to broadening the base of a pyramid; it allows businesses to build upon established foundations while exploring new markets or customer segments.

A classic example of horizontal progress is the evolution of fast food chains. Companies like McDonald's have not only expanded their menu offerings but have also entered new geographical markets and adapted their services to cater to local tastes. By leveraging their existing brand recognition and operational efficiencies, these companies can achieve growth without needing to reinvent the wheel.

Horizontal progress often requires less risk compared to vertical progress since it builds on proven concepts. Businesses can analyze existing market trends, consumer preferences, and competitive landscapes to identify opportunities for expansion. This approach allows for incremental improvements that can lead to enhanced customer satisfaction and loyalty. Moreover, horizontal progress can create synergies within an organization, enabling it to optimize resources and maximize profitability.

The Synergy Between Vertical and Horizontal Progress

While vertical and horizontal progress may seem like opposing strategies, they are not mutually exclusive. In fact, successful businesses often find ways to integrate both approaches into their growth strategies. Companies that excel at horizontal expansion can create a robust platform upon which vertical innovations can flourish.

For example, consider a technology company that has established itself in the software market through horizontal progress by offering various applications for different industries. Once the company has built a solid customer base and brand reputation, it may leverage this foundation to explore vertical innovations—developing entirely new software solutions that address emerging needs or challenges in the market.

This synergy allows businesses to mitigate risks associated with vertical innovations while capitalizing on the strengths of horizontal growth. By fostering an environment where both types of progress are valued, organizations can create a culture of continuous improvement and innovation.

Identifying Lucrative Ideas

When it comes to discovering lucrative ideas, entrepreneurs must carefully evaluate their goals and resources to determine which path—vertical or horizontal—aligns best with their vision. Here are some considerations for each approach:

1. **Market Analysis**: Entrepreneurs should conduct thorough market research to identify gaps in existing offerings or areas where consumer needs are not being met. Vertical progress may be warranted if there is a clear demand for groundbreaking solutions. Conversely, horizontal progress may be more suitable if opportunities exist for enhancing current products or services.

2. **Resource Allocation**: Vertical innovations often require significant investments in R&D, talent acquisition, and technology development. Entrepreneurs should assess whether they have the necessary resources to pursue high-risk ventures. In contrast, horizontal progress may demand less upfront investment, making it more accessible for startups or smaller businesses.

3. **Risk Tolerance**: Understanding one's risk appetite is crucial when deciding between vertical and horizontal progress. Entrepreneurs comfortable with uncertainty may be more inclined to pursue vertical innovations that could yield transformative results. Those who prefer stability may find greater success in refining existing concepts through horizontal expansion.

4. **Long-Term Vision**: Finally, entrepreneurs should align their choice with their long-term vision for their business. If the goal is to disrupt an industry and establish a pioneering legacy, vertical progress may be the right path. However, if the aim is to build a sustainable business model with steady growth, horizontal progress could offer a more pragmatic approach.

In conclusion, both vertical and horizontal progress play vital roles in the landscape of innovation and entrepreneurship. Understanding the differences between these approaches enables aspiring entrepreneurs to make informed decisions about how to develop their ideas and grow their businesses. While vertical progress embodies the spirit of invention and transformation, horizontal progress emphasizes refinement and expansion.

Ultimately, the most successful innovators will recognize the value of both paths and seek opportunities to integrate them into their strategies. By balancing the ambition of creating something entirely new with the practicality of enhancing what already exists, entrepreneurs can navigate the complexities of the market and uncover lucrative ideas that drive lasting success.

Chapter 2

Monopoly vs. Competition

In the sphere of economics and business, the concepts of monopoly and competition represent two distinct market structures that significantly influence how industries operate, how businesses strategize, and ultimately, how consumers experience products and services. While competition is often lauded for fostering innovation and providing choices, monopolies can offer unique advantages that can lead to stability and efficiency. This chapter looks into the characteristics of each market structure, highlighting the benefits of monopolies while examining the drawbacks associated with competition.

Understanding Monopoly

A monopoly exists when a single company or entity dominates a particular market, controlling a substantial share of the supply for a good or service. This dominance can arise from various factors, including exclusive access to resources, government regulations, or technological superiority. In a monopolistic market, the monopolist has significant pricing power, allowing it to set prices above competitive levels without losing customers.

It should also be understood that most successful companies always aim for monopoly by creating unique

products or services. They have advantage to set their own prices and maintain higher profits that keep them afloat and leading in business.
However, competitions among other companies always amount to a race to the bottom and exitinction.

Benefits of Monopolies

1. **Economies of Scale**: One of the most significant advantages of monopolies is their ability to achieve economies of scale. As a single entity produces a large volume of goods or services, it can spread its fixed costs over a broader output base. This efficiency often results in lower production costs per unit, allowing the monopolist to maintain higher profit margins. For instance, utility companies often operate as monopolies because they can deliver services more efficiently than multiple competing firms could.

2. **Consistent Quality**: Monopolies can provide a consistent level of quality across their offerings. With no competition to undercut them, monopolists are incentivized to maintain high standards to retain customer loyalty. This stability can be particularly beneficial in industries where quality is paramount, such as pharmaceuticals or aerospace, where rigorous standards are crucial for safety and efficacy.

3. **Long-term Investment in Innovation**: While competition is often credited with driving innovation, monopolies can also invest heavily in research and development (R&D) without the immediate pressure of competitors. With guaranteed market dominance and profits, monopolists may allocate substantial resources toward groundbreaking technologies and innovations. For example, companies like Google have leveraged their monopolistic position in search engines to invest in artificial intelligence and other advanced technologies that may not have been feasible in a highly competitive environment.

4. **Stability in Pricing**: Monopolies typically result in more stable pricing compared to competitive markets. In competitive environments, prices can fluctuate dramatically due to supply and demand dynamics. Conversely, monopolists can set prices that reflect their cost structure and profit objectives, reducing price volatility for consumers. This predictability can be advantageous for both consumers and businesses when planning budgets and expenditures.

The Drawbacks of Competition

While competition is often viewed as beneficial for driving innovation and consumer choice, it also comes with several drawbacks that can negatively impact both businesses and consumers.

1. **Market Saturation**: In highly competitive markets, the presence of numerous players can lead to market saturation. As businesses vie for market share, they may oversupply products or services, leading to diminished profit margins. This saturation can ultimately result in business failures, job losses, and economic instability within the industry.

2. **Short-term Focus**: Competing firms often prioritize short-term gains over long-term sustainability due to the pressure to outperform rivals. This focus on immediate profits can stifle innovation and discourage investments in R&D, as companies may be reluctant to allocate resources toward projects with uncertain payoffs. Consequently, industries may miss out on transformative innovations that could benefit society as a whole.

3. **Price Wars**: Competition can lead to destructive price wars where companies continuously undercut each other's prices to attract customers. While this may benefit consumers in the short term through lower prices, it can jeopardize the financial health of businesses, leading to reduced quality of products and services as firms struggle to maintain profitability. In extreme cases, this can result in companies exiting the market altogether.

4. **Inefficiencies**: In a competitive landscape, businesses may duplicate efforts in marketing,

distribution, and production processes to differentiate themselves from rivals. This redundancy can lead to inefficiencies within the industry as resources are wasted on overlapping initiatives rather than being utilized for innovation or improvement.

Finding Balance

While both monopolies and competition have their respective advantages and drawbacks, it is essential to recognize that neither extreme is ideal for all industries or situations. A balanced approach that incorporates elements of both structures may yield the best outcomes for consumers and businesses alike.

Regulatory frameworks can play a vital role in ensuring that monopolies do not exploit their market power at the expense of consumers while still allowing them the freedom to innovate and invest in long-term projects. On the other hand, fostering healthy competition through antitrust laws can prevent market saturation and encourage sustainable practices among businesses.

In conclusion, the dichotomy between monopoly and competition presents a complex landscape for businesses and consumers alike. Monopolies offer distinct advantages such as economies of scale, consistent quality, long-term investment potential, and pricing stability. However, competition also serves an essential purpose by driving innovation and providing consumer choices. Understanding these dynamics allows stakeholders to navigate the intricacies of market structures effectively, paving the way for a more balanced economic environment that fosters both innovation and consumer welfare. Ultimately, striking the right balance between monopolistic advantages and competitive pressures may lead to optimal outcomes for all parties involved in the marketplace.

Chapter 3:

The Power of Technology

Driving Advancement and Fostering Innovation

In the modern world, technology stands as a pivotal force that shapes not only economies but also societies and cultures. From the dawn of the industrial revolution to the digital age, technological advancements have transformed how we live, work, and interact with one another. This chapter explores the multifaceted power of technology, examining how it drives advancement and fosters innovation across various sectors, ultimately reshaping the human experience.

Technology is Paramount and is a crucial driver of progress and must be leveraged to create significant advancement.

The Catalyst for Change

At its core, technology serves as a catalyst for change. It enables us to solve complex problems, streamline processes, and enhance productivity. The advent of the internet revolutionized communication, breaking down geographical barriers and allowing instant information exchange. This connectivity has led to the emergence of global markets, enabling businesses to operate beyond borders and foster international collaboration.

For instance, consider the rise of e-commerce platforms like Amazon and Alibaba. These companies have transformed retail by leveraging technology to connect buyers and sellers worldwide. By utilizing data analytics, they can personalize shopping experiences, predict consumer behavior, and optimize supply chains. This technological integration not only drives economic growth but also empowers consumers with unprecedented choices and convenience.

Innovation Through Collaboration

Technology thrives on collaboration, often bringing together diverse perspectives to spark innovation. The rise of open-source software is a prime example of this phenomenon. Developers from around the globe contribute to projects like Linux or Apache, sharing knowledge and resources to create robust solutions that benefit everyone. This collaborative spirit fosters an environment where innovation flourishes, as individuals build upon each other's ideas rather than competing in isolation.

Moreover, technology has facilitated interdisciplinary collaboration across various fields. In healthcare, for instance, medical professionals, engineers, and data scientists work together to develop cutting-edge solutions such as telemedicine platforms and wearable health devices. These innovations not only improve patient outcomes but also make healthcare more accessible, particularly in underserved regions.

Automation and Efficiency

One of the most significant impacts of technology is its ability to automate repetitive tasks, leading to enhanced efficiency in various industries. Automation technologies, such as robotics and artificial intelligence (AI), have transformed manufacturing processes by reducing human error and increasing production speed. Factories equipped with robotic arms can produce goods with precision and consistency, allowing companies to meet rising consumer demands while minimizing costs.

In addition to manufacturing, automation is reshaping sectors like agriculture. Precision farming techniques utilize drones and sensors to monitor crop health, optimize irrigation, and manage resources effectively. By harnessing technology, farmers can increase yields while reducing environmental impact—a crucial consideration in an era of climate change.

Driving Sustainable Solutions

As global challenges such as climate change and resource scarcity intensify, technology plays a vital role in driving sustainable solutions. Renewable energy technologies, such as solar panels and wind turbines, have gained traction as viable alternatives to fossil fuels. Innovations in energy storage, like advanced batteries, enable us to harness renewable energy more effectively, ensuring a stable power supply even when conditions are less than ideal.

Furthermore, technology is pivotal in promoting sustainable practices within industries. The rise of smart cities—urban areas that leverage IoT (Internet of Things) technology—demonstrates how data-driven solutions can enhance urban living. Smart traffic management systems reduce congestion and emissions, while

intelligent waste management systems optimize resource use. By integrating technology into our cities, we can create more sustainable environments for future generations.

Empowering Individuals

The power of technology extends beyond businesses and industries; it also empowers individuals. The proliferation of smartphones and internet access has democratized information, allowing people to educate themselves and access resources previously unavailable. Online learning platforms like Coursera and Khan Academy enable learners from all walks of life to acquire new skills and knowledge at their own pace.

Social media platforms have further amplified individual voices, enabling grassroots movements to gain momentum and effect change. From environmental activism to social justice campaigns, technology has provided a platform for marginalized communities to share their stories and mobilize support on a global scale.

Challenges and Ethical Considerations

Despite its many benefits, the rapid advancement of technology also presents challenges that warrant careful consideration. Issues such as data privacy, cybersecurity threats, and the digital divide highlight the need for responsible innovation. As organizations increasingly rely on data-driven decision-making, ensuring the ethical use of personal information becomes paramount.

Moreover, the rise of automation raises concerns about job displacement. While technology creates new opportunities, it can also render certain jobs obsolete. It is essential for policymakers and businesses to collaborate on reskilling initiatives that prepare the workforce for the jobs of tomorrow.

The power of technology is undeniable; it drives advancement and fosters innovation in ways that continuously reshape our world. From enhancing efficiency in industries to empowering individuals through access to information, technology plays a crucial role in addressing complex challenges and creating opportunities for growth.

As we move forward into an increasingly interconnected future, harnessing the potential of technology responsibly will be vital. By embracing collaboration, prioritizing sustainability, and addressing ethical considerations, we can ensure that technology serves as a force for good—one that uplifts societies and fosters innovation for generations to come. In this dynamic landscape, the true power of technology lies not just in its capabilities but in our collective ability to wield it wisely for the betterment of humanity.

Chapter 4:

The Importance of a Strong Founding Team

The Critical Role of a Unified Team in Overcoming Obstacles

In the realm of startups and entrepreneurial ventures, the significance of a strong founding team cannot be overstated. While innovative ideas and adequate funding are essential for success, it is often the strength and cohesion of the founding team that determines whether a venture will thrive or falter. This chapter expains the critical role of a unified team in overcoming obstacles, highlighting key attributes that contribute to a strong founding team and illustrating how collaboration can lead to resilience and success.

The Foundation of Success

A strong founding team serves as the backbone of any startup. Each member brings unique skills, perspectives, and experiences that contribute to the collective strength of the group. This diversity is crucial; it allows the team to approach challenges from multiple angles, fostering creativity and innovation. When members complement each other's strengths and weaknesses, they create a well-rounded unit capable of tackling complex problems.

For example, consider a tech startup aiming to develop a groundbreaking software application. A successful team might comprise a visionary product manager, a skilled developer, a savvy marketer, and a financial expert. Each member plays a distinct role, yet their collaborative efforts drive the project forward. When faced with obstacles—be it technical challenges, market competition, or funding issues—the team can draw on their collective expertise to devise effective solutions.

Building Trust and Communication

Trust is the cornerstone of any effective team. A unified founding team cultivates an environment where members feel safe to express their ideas, voice concerns, and challenge one another constructively. Open communication fosters transparency, ensuring that everyone is aligned with the team's goals and vision. When team members trust one another, they are more likely to take risks and innovate without fear of failure.

Moreover, effective communication is vital for navigating obstacles. In times of crisis or uncertainty, a cohesive team can quickly mobilize resources and brainstorm solutions. For instance, during the COVID-19 pandemic, many startups faced unprecedented challenges. Teams that communicated openly about their struggles were better equipped to pivot their business models or explore new markets. This adaptability is often what separates successful ventures from those that succumb to pressure.

Resilience in the Face of Adversity

The entrepreneurial journey is fraught with obstacles—financial constraints, market fluctuations, regulatory hurdles, and competition are just a few of the challenges that founders face. A strong founding team provides the resilience needed to navigate these difficulties. When setbacks occur, a unified team can rally together, drawing on their shared commitment to overcome adversity.

For instance, consider a startup that experiences a significant setback due to product failure or negative customer feedback. A cohesive team can analyze the situation collectively, identify areas for improvement, and implement changes swiftly. This resilience not only helps the startup recover but also strengthens the bond among team members. Shared experiences of overcoming challenges can foster camaraderie and enhance teamwork.

Shared Vision and Goals

A unified founding team operates with a shared vision and common goals. When every member understands and believes in the mission of the venture, they are more motivated to contribute their best efforts. This alignment is crucial for maintaining focus during challenging times when distractions and uncertainties abound.

Establishing clear goals helps the team prioritize tasks and allocate resources effectively. For example, if a startup aims to launch its product within six months, each member must understand their role in achieving that deadline. Regular check-ins and updates keep everyone accountable and ensure that progress is being made toward the shared objective. When all members are pulling in the same direction, obstacles become manageable rather than insurmountable.

Conflict Resolution and Problem-Solving

Conflict is an inevitable part of any collaborative effort, particularly in high-stakes environments like startups. However, a strong founding team views conflict as an opportunity for growth rather than a roadblock. When team members approach disagreements with respect and openness, they can engage in constructive dialogues that lead to innovative solutions.

Effective conflict resolution involves active listening and empathy. Team members must be willing to understand differing viewpoints and find common ground. For instance, if there's a disagreement about product features, rather than allowing tensions to escalate, the team can hold a brainstorming session to explore all perspectives. This collaborative approach often results in more robust solutions that reflect the collective wisdom of the group.

Leadership and Empowerment

Strong leadership within a founding team is essential for guiding the group through challenges. Effective leaders inspire trust and motivate team members to take ownership of their roles. They foster an environment where individuals feel empowered to contribute their ideas and take initiative.

Moreover, leadership within a unified team is not limited to one person; it can be distributed among members based on expertise or situational needs. This shared leadership model encourages accountability and allows for agile decision-making. For example, if a technical challenge arises, the developer may take the lead in proposing solutions while others support by providing insights from their respective areas.

The importance of a strong founding team cannot be overstated in the journey of entrepreneurship. A unified team equipped with diverse skills, open communication, trust, resilience, shared vision, effective conflict resolution, and strong leadership is better positioned to overcome obstacles than any individual working alone.

As startups navigate the complexities of launching and scaling their ventures, investing in building a cohesive founding team should be a top priority. By fostering collaboration and creating an environment where every member feels valued and empowered, entrepreneurs can not only tackle challenges head-on but also create a culture of innovation that drives long-term success.

In essence, while obstacles are an inherent part of any entrepreneurial endeavor, it is the strength of the founding team that ultimately determines whether those obstacles become stepping stones or stumbling blocks on the path to success.

Chapter 5

Sales and Distribution Matter

In the competitive landscape of business, the success of a product or service is not solely determined by its quality or innovation; it is equally influenced by effective sales and distribution strategies. This chapter explores the critical importance of sales techniques in conjunction with product development, strategic marketing approaches, and optimizing the sales process to maximize reach and profitability.

The Interplay Between Sales and Product Development

Effective sales techniques are intrinsically linked to product development. The relationship between these two functions is symbiotic; while product development focuses on creating a solution that meets customer needs, sales teams are responsible for communicating that value to potential buyers. Understanding this interplay is essential for achieving market success.

1. **Feedback Loop**: Sales teams are often the first point of contact with customers. They gather valuable insights about customer preferences, pain points, and market trends. This feedback can inform product development, ensuring that future iterations or new products align with

customer expectations. For example, if a sales representative learns that customers struggle with a specific feature, the product development team can prioritize enhancements to address this issue.

2. **Value Proposition**: Effective sales techniques emphasize the importance of articulating a compelling value proposition. A well-defined value proposition outlines how a product solves a problem or improves the customer's situation. It is crucial for sales teams to collaborate closely with product developers to ensure they fully understand the product's benefits and can communicate them effectively. This alignment helps create a consistent message across all touchpoints, enhancing credibility and trust.

3. **Target Market Alignment**: Successful product development requires a clear understanding of the target market. Sales teams play a pivotal role in identifying and refining target demographics based on their interactions with customers. By sharing this information with product developers, sales teams can help shape products that not only meet market demands but also resonate with specific customer segments.

Strategic Marketing Approaches

Strategic marketing is vital for driving sales and ensuring that products reach their intended audience. A well-crafted marketing strategy integrates various elements, including market research, branding, positioning, and promotional tactics.

1. **Market Research**: Understanding the market landscape is the foundation of any successful marketing strategy. Conducting thorough market research allows businesses to identify trends, assess competition, and understand customer preferences. This information is invaluable for both sales and product development teams. For instance, if market research indicates a growing demand for eco-friendly products, businesses can adapt their offerings accordingly and tailor their sales pitches to highlight sustainability features.

2. **Brand Positioning**: Brand positioning refers to how a brand is perceived in relation to its competitors. A strong brand position differentiates a company in the marketplace and influences customer purchasing decisions. Sales teams must be well-versed in the brand's positioning to effectively convey its unique attributes during interactions with potential buyers. Consistent messaging across marketing channels reinforces brand identity and builds customer loyalty.

3. **Integrated Marketing Campaigns**: An integrated marketing campaign combines various promotional tactics—such as digital marketing, social media, public relations, and events—to create a cohesive message that resonates with the target audience. Sales teams benefit from integrated campaigns as they provide multiple touchpoints for engagement. For example, if a

company launches a new product through an online campaign, sales representatives can follow up with leads generated from that campaign to convert interest into sales.

4. **Content Marketing**: Content marketing plays a crucial role in establishing thought leadership and educating potential customers about a product or service. By producing high-quality content—such as blog posts, whitepapers, or videos—businesses can attract and engage their target audience. Sales teams can leverage this content during their outreach efforts, using it as a tool to nurture leads and build relationships.

Optimizing the Sales Process

An optimized sales process is essential for maximizing efficiency and closing deals effectively. Streamlining the sales process involves analyzing each stage of the sales funnel, identifying bottlenecks, and implementing strategies to improve performance.

1. **Sales Funnel Analysis**: The sales funnel represents the journey potential customers take from awareness to purchase. Analyzing each stage—awareness, interest, consideration, intent, evaluation, and purchase—allows businesses to pinpoint areas for improvement. For example, if a significant number of leads drop off during the consideration phase, it may indicate that the sales

team needs to provide more information or address specific concerns.

2. **Lead Qualification**: Not all leads are created equal; some are more likely to convert than others. Implementing a lead qualification process helps prioritize high-potential leads based on criteria such as budget, authority, need, and timeline (BANT). By focusing on qualified leads, sales teams can allocate their time and resources more effectively, increasing the likelihood of closing deals.

3. **Sales Enablement Tools**: Technology plays a pivotal role in optimizing the sales process. Sales enablement tools—such as Customer Relationship Management (CRM) systems, analytics platforms, and communication tools—equip sales teams with the resources they need to succeed. These tools facilitate better tracking of customer interactions, streamline communication, and provide valuable data insights that inform decision-making.

4. **Training and Development**: Continuous training and development are essential for keeping sales teams equipped with the latest techniques and industry knowledge. Regular training sessions can enhance skills in areas such as negotiation, objection handling, and relationship building. Investing in professional development not only boosts individual performance but also fosters a culture of excellence within the sales team.

5. **Customer Relationship Management**: Building strong relationships with customers is crucial for long-term success. A focus on customer relationship management (CRM) involves nurturing leads through personalized communication and follow-ups. Sales teams should prioritize understanding customer needs and preferences to tailor their approach accordingly. This relationship-building fosters loyalty and increases the likelihood of repeat business.

6. **Performance Metrics**: Establishing key performance indicators (KPIs) allows businesses to measure the effectiveness of their sales strategies. Metrics such as conversion rates, average deal size, and sales cycle length provide valuable insights into performance trends and areas for improvement. Regularly reviewing these metrics enables teams to adjust their strategies in real-time to achieve better results.

In conclusion, effective sales techniques are paramount for translating innovative products into market success. The interplay between sales and product development ensures that offerings align with customer needs while strategic marketing approaches amplify reach and engagement. Optimizing the sales process through analysis, lead qualification, technology integration, training, relationship management, and performance metrics ultimately drives revenue growth.

As businesses navigate an increasingly competitive landscape, prioritizing sales and distribution strategies will be essential for sustaining success. By fostering collaboration between sales teams and product developers while implementing strategic marketing initiatives and optimizing processes, organizations can create a robust framework for achieving their goals and delivering value to customers. In this dynamic environment, those who master the art of selling will not only survive but thrive in their respective markets.

Chapter 6

The Future of Startups

The landscape of startups is evolving rapidly, driven by technological advancements, shifting consumer preferences, and a global focus on sustainability. As we look toward the future, several key trends will shape the startup ecosystem, presenting both challenges and opportunities for entrepreneurs.

1. Emphasis on Sustainability

The future of startups will be heavily influenced by the growing demand for sustainable practices. Consumers are increasingly prioritizing eco-friendly products and services, prompting startups to incorporate sustainability into their business models. Entrepreneurs who focus on reducing their environmental impact and promoting social responsibility will not only attract a loyal customer base but also position themselves favorably in a competitive market. Innovations in renewable energy, waste reduction, and circular economy models will be at the forefront of this movement.

2. Technological Integration

Technology will continue to be a driving force behind startup growth. Emerging technologies like artificial intelligence (AI), blockchain, and the Internet of Things

(IoT) are transforming industries and creating new business opportunities. Startups that leverage these technologies can enhance efficiency, improve customer experiences, and disrupt traditional markets. For instance, AI-powered analytics can provide valuable insights into consumer behavior, enabling startups to tailor their offerings more effectively.

3. Remote Work and Global Talent

The COVID-19 pandemic has accelerated the shift toward remote work, and this trend is likely to persist. Startups can tap into a global talent pool, allowing them to hire the best minds regardless of geographical location. This flexibility not only reduces overhead costs but also fosters diversity within teams, driving innovation and creativity. However, startups must also invest in effective communication tools and company culture to maintain cohesion among remote employees.

4. Access to Funding

The funding landscape for startups is evolving as well. Traditional venture capital is being complemented by alternative funding sources such as crowdfunding, angel investors, and revenue-based financing. This diversification allows startups to explore various avenues for securing capital, making it easier for innovative ideas to find support. Additionally, the rise of impact investing—where investors seek social and environmental returns alongside financial gains—will encourage more startups focused on purpose-driven missions.

The future of startups is bright, characterized by a commitment to sustainability, technological integration, remote work flexibility, and diverse funding options. Entrepreneurs who embrace these trends will be well-positioned to navigate the complexities of the modern marketplace and create lasting impact. As we move forward, adaptability and innovation will remain the cornerstones of successful startups in an ever-changing world.

The Impact of Innovative Startups on Future Development Through New Technologies

In an era marked by rapid technological advancement, innovative startups are increasingly becoming the engines of economic growth and societal change. Unlike traditional companies that often focus on improving existing technologies, many startups are dedicated to creating entirely new technologies. This approach not only drives innovation but also shapes the future landscape of industries, economies, and everyday life.

1. Disruption Through Novel Solutions

Innovative startups are uniquely positioned to disrupt established markets by introducing groundbreaking solutions that challenge the status quo. For instance, companies like SpaceX and Blue Origin have revolutionized the aerospace industry by developing reusable rocket technology, significantly reducing the cost of space travel. This paradigm shift opens up new possibilities for satellite deployment, space tourism, and even planetary exploration. Such innovations not only create new markets but also inspire further advancements across various sectors, including telecommunications and environmental science.

2. Fostering a Culture of Experimentation

Startups often operate with a culture of experimentation, allowing them to explore uncharted territories without the constraints faced by larger corporations. This agility enables them to pivot quickly based on market feedback, leading to the rapid development of novel technologies. For example, companies like Impossible Foods and Beyond Meat have pioneered plant-based meat alternatives that cater to the growing demand for sustainable food sources. Their focus on innovation rather than mere improvement has spurred interest in alternative proteins, prompting traditional food companies to invest in similar technologies, thereby accelerating the overall shift towards sustainable food systems.

3. Addressing Global Challenges

Innovative startups are also at the forefront of addressing pressing global challenges through new technologies. Climate change, healthcare access, and education disparities are just a few areas where startups are making significant contributions. For instance, companies like Tesla have not only improved electric vehicle technology but have also introduced energy storage solutions and solar products that aim to create a sustainable energy ecosystem. By developing new technologies that address these critical issues, startups can influence policy decisions and encourage investment in sustainability initiatives.

4. Collaboration and Ecosystem Building

The rise of innovative startups is fostering collaboration within ecosystems that encourage knowledge sharing and co-development of new technologies. Incubators and accelerators play a crucial role in this process by providing resources, mentorship, and networking opportunities for emerging entrepreneurs. Programs like Y Combinator and Techstars have successfully launched numerous startups that focus on creating new technologies across various sectors, from fintech to healthtech. These collaborative environments not only enhance innovation but also create a supportive infrastructure for startups to thrive.

5. The Role of Emerging Technologies

Emerging technologies such as artificial intelligence (AI), blockchain, and quantum computing are being harnessed by innovative startups to create new solutions that were previously unimaginable. For instance, AI-driven startups like OpenAI are pushing the boundaries of machine learning to develop applications that can understand and generate human-like text, revolutionizing industries such as content creation and customer service. Similarly, blockchain startups are introducing decentralized finance (DeFi) platforms that challenge traditional banking systems by offering transparent and secure financial services. These advancements highlight how startups are not merely improving existing technologies but are instead redefining the technological landscape.

6. Economic Growth and Job Creation

The focus on creating new technologies positions innovative startups as vital contributors to economic growth and job creation. As these companies emerge and scale, they generate employment opportunities in high-tech fields and stimulate demand for skilled labor. According to the World Economic Forum (2021), technology-driven startups are projected to create millions of jobs globally in the coming years as they expand their operations and develop new products. This growth not only benefits the economy but also fosters a dynamic workforce equipped with cutting-edge skills.

Conclusion

Innovative startups are set to play a pivotal role in shaping future development by focusing on creating new technologies rather than simply improving existing ones. Their ability to disrupt markets, foster experimentation, address global challenges, build collaborative ecosystems, leverage emerging technologies, and drive economic growth positions them as key players in the 21st-century landscape. As these startups continue to innovate, they will not only redefine industries but also contribute significantly to a more sustainable and equitable future.

What you need to know to stand out

To stand out as an entrepreneur in today's competitive landscape, it's essential to embrace a unique blend of creativity, resilience, and strategic thinking.
First, identify your niche—understand what sets your business apart from others. This could be an innovative product, exceptional customer service, or a sustainable approach.

Conduct thorough market research to pinpoint gaps and opportunities that resonate with your target audience.

Next, cultivate a strong personal brand. Your story, values, and vision should be authentic and relatable, helping customers connect with you on a deeper level. Leverage social media to share your journey and engage with potential clients, building a community around your brand.

Networking is also crucial. Surround yourself with mentors and fellow entrepreneurs who can provide guidance and support. Attend industry events, join local business groups, and seek collaborations that enhance your visibility.

Finally, prioritize adaptability. The business landscape is ever-changing; being open to feedback and willing to pivot your strategies can set you apart.

Embrace innovation and stay ahead of trends to keep your offerings relevant.

By focusing on these key areas—niche identification, personal branding, networking, and adaptability—you'll not only stand out but also lay a solid foundation for sustainable growth and success in your entrepreneurial journey.

Mistakes to avoid when starting a business

Starting a business can be an exhilarating yet challenging journey. To enhance your chances of success, it's crucial to avoid common pitfalls. Here are some mistakes to steer clear of:

1. **Neglecting Market Research**: Failing to understand your target audience and market trends can lead to misguided decisions. Conduct thorough research to identify customer needs, preferences, and potential competitors.

2. **Underestimating Financial Needs**: Many entrepreneurs overlook the importance of a detailed financial plan. Ensure you have enough capital not only for startup costs but also for sustaining operations until your business becomes profitable.

3. **Lack of a Clear Business Plan**: A well-structured business plan serves as a roadmap for your venture. It outlines your goals, strategies, and the steps needed to achieve them. Avoid starting without this essential document.

4. **Ignoring Legal Requirements**: Compliance with local laws and regulations is critical. Failing to register your business, obtain necessary licenses, or adhere to tax obligations can lead to costly legal issues down the road.

5. **Trying to Do Everything Alone**: Entrepreneurs often feel the need to handle every aspect of the business themselves. However, delegating tasks and seeking advice from experienced professionals can lead to better decision-making and efficiency.

6. **Neglecting Marketing Efforts**: Even the best products need visibility. Develop a marketing strategy that effectively promotes your brand and engages potential customers across various channels.

By avoiding these mistakes, you can lay a solid foundation for your business and increase your chances of long-term success. Remember, learning from others' experiences can save you time, money, and frustration in your entrepreneurial journey.

Chapter 7

Contrarian Thinking

The Significance of Challenging Conventional Beliefs

The present world is saturated with information and conventional wisdom, the ability to think contrarian—challenging established beliefs and norms—has become a vital skill for identifying unique opportunities. Contrarian thinking is not merely about being different for the sake of it; rather, it involves a disciplined approach to questioning assumptions and exploring alternative perspectives. This chapter looks into the significance of contrarian thinking, its role in fostering independent thought, and how it can lead to discovering innovative opportunities.

Understanding Contrarian Thinking

At its core, contrarian thinking is about skepticism toward the status quo. It requires individuals to step back from mainstream narratives and critically evaluate widely accepted beliefs. This mindset is crucial in various contexts, from investing and business to personal development and social issues. By questioning conventional wisdom, contrarians often uncover insights that others overlook, enabling them to make informed decisions based on a more comprehensive understanding of the landscape.

The Power of Questioning Assumptions

One of the first steps in contrarian thinking is recognizing the assumptions that underpin conventional beliefs. These assumptions often go unchallenged, leading to a herd mentality where individuals follow the crowd without critical evaluation. For example, in the investment world, many investors flock to popular stocks during market booms, believing that past performance guarantees future success. However, contrarian investors might analyze market trends differently, identifying undervalued stocks that others have dismissed.

By questioning these assumptions, contrarians can identify discrepancies between perception and reality. This critical analysis allows them to spot opportunities that others may miss. For instance, during economic downturns, contrarian investors might see potential in distressed assets while others retreat in fear. This ability to see value where others see risk is a hallmark of successful contrarian thinking.

Cultivating Independent Thought

Contrarian thinking fosters independent thought, encouraging individuals to develop their own perspectives rather than relying on the opinions of others. In an age dominated by social media and instant information dissemination, it is easy to fall into the trap of echo chambers where only prevailing opinions are reinforced. Contrarians actively seek diverse viewpoints, engaging with ideas that challenge their beliefs.

This independent thought process is essential for innovation. Many groundbreaking ideas have emerged from individuals who dared to think differently. For example, Steve Jobs and Apple revolutionized personal computing and mobile technology by defying conventional design principles. Instead of following existing trends, Jobs focused on creating user-friendly products that prioritized aesthetics and functionality, ultimately reshaping entire industries.

Identifying Unique Opportunities

Contrarian thinking equips individuals with the tools to identify unique opportunities that arise from unconventional insights. By looking beyond surface-level trends and questioning prevailing narratives, contrarians can spot gaps in the market that others overlook. This approach is particularly valuable in entrepreneurship and investment, where recognizing unmet needs can lead to significant rewards.

Consider the rise of remote work technologies during the COVID-19 pandemic. While many businesses were hesitant to embrace remote work as a long-term solution, contrarian thinkers saw an opportunity to innovate in this space. Companies that developed collaboration tools and virtual communication platforms thrived as organizations adapted to new ways of working. Those who recognized the potential early on were able to capitalize on a shift that many had dismissed as temporary.

Embracing Failure as a Learning Tool

A key aspect of contrarian thinking is embracing failure as a valuable learning experience. Conventional wisdom often promotes a fear of failure, leading individuals to avoid risks and stick with what is familiar. In contrast, contrarians understand that failure can provide critical insights that inform future decisions.

For instance, Thomas Edison famously failed thousands of times before successfully inventing the light bulb. Each failure taught him something new about materials and electrical systems, ultimately leading to his groundbreaking invention. By reframing failure as a stepping stone rather than a setback, contrarians cultivate resilience and adaptability—traits essential for navigating uncertain environments.

The Role of Curiosity

Curiosity is another cornerstone of contrarian thinking. A genuine desire to learn and explore new ideas fuels the willingness to challenge conventional beliefs. Curiosity drives individuals to ask "why" and "what if," prompting deeper exploration of topics that others may take for granted.

This inquisitive nature often leads to unexpected discoveries. For instance, in the realm of science, many breakthroughs have occurred when researchers questioned established theories. The discovery of penicillin by Alexander Fleming was serendipitous; his curiosity about mold led him to explore its antibacterial properties, ultimately transforming medicine.

Building a Contrarian Mindset

Developing a contrarian mindset requires practice and intentionality. Here are some strategies for cultivating this way of thinking:

1. **Challenge Assumptions**: Regularly question your beliefs and those of others. Ask yourself what evidence supports these beliefs and whether alternative explanations exist.

2. **Seek Diverse Perspectives**: Engage with people who hold different views. This exposure will broaden your understanding and help you recognize blind spots in your thinking.

3. **Embrace Uncertainty**: Accept that uncertainty is part of the decision-making process. Use it as an opportunity to explore various scenarios rather than relying solely on established norms.

4. **Reflect on Failures**: Analyze past failures objectively to extract valuable lessons. Consider how these experiences can inform your future decisions.

5. **Cultivate Curiosity**: Foster a habit of lifelong learning by exploring new topics and asking questions that challenge conventional wisdom.

Contrarian thinking is an invaluable asset in today's fast-paced world, where conventional beliefs often dictate actions and decisions. By challenging these norms and fostering independent thought, individuals can identify unique opportunities that lead to innovation and growth. Embracing failure as a learning tool and nurturing curiosity further enhances this mindset, allowing for continuous exploration and discovery.

As we navigate an increasingly complex landscape, cultivating a contrarian approach will empower us to break free from the confines of conventional wisdom, ultimately leading to richer insights and transformative opportunities. In doing so, we not only enhance our own potential but also contribute to a culture of innovation that benefits society as a whole.

Chapter 8

The Role of Secrets

The Value of Undiscovered Insights and Untapped Potentials in Successful Startups

In the dynamic landscape of entrepreneurship, the allure of secrets—those undiscovered insights and untapped potentials—can often be the catalyst for groundbreaking success. Secrets in this context refer to unique knowledge, innovative ideas, or hidden market opportunities that have yet to be recognized or exploited. Understanding the role of these secrets is crucial for entrepreneurs aiming to carve out their niche in a competitive environment. This chapter explores how secrets contribute to startup success, the importance of recognizing and leveraging them, and the ethical considerations that accompany this pursuit.

The Power of Undiscovered Insights

Undiscovered insights are the gems hidden within the complexities of market dynamics, consumer behavior, and technological advancements. These insights can often lead to innovative solutions that address unmet needs, creating a competitive advantage for startups. For instance, Airbnb emerged from the simple yet profound realization that travelers were seeking affordable and authentic accommodation options beyond traditional hotels. The founders recognized a gap in the market that others had overlooked, transforming a modest idea into a multi-billion-dollar enterprise.

The importance of these insights cannot be overstated. Startups that succeed often do so because they have identified a unique angle or perspective that differentiates them from established players. This differentiation can stem from a variety of sources, including personal experiences, industry observations, or even serendipitous discoveries. The key lies in an entrepreneur's ability to remain observant and open-minded, allowing them to recognize potential where others see only noise.

Untapped Potentials: A Goldmine for Entrepreneurs

Untapped potentials represent the latent capabilities within individuals, teams, or markets that have not yet been fully realized. For startups, harnessing these potentials can lead to innovative products and services that resonate with consumers. Consider the rise of social media platforms; many entrepreneurs tapped into the untapped potential of online connectivity and community-building, creating platforms that revolutionized communication.

A prime example is Instagram, which initially began as a simple photo-sharing app. The founders recognized the untapped potential of visual storytelling and social interaction, which led to the platform's rapid growth and eventual acquisition by Facebook. By focusing on a specific niche—sharing moments through images—they created a space that fulfilled a growing demand for visual content.

Identifying untapped potentials requires a keen understanding of market trends and consumer psychology. Entrepreneurs must ask themselves critical questions: What needs are currently unmet? What frustrations do consumers experience with existing solutions? By exploring these questions, startups can uncover opportunities that may not be immediately apparent.

The Ethical Dimension of Secrets

While secrets can serve as powerful drivers of innovation and success, it is essential to approach them with ethical considerations in mind. The pursuit of undiscovered insights should not come at the expense of integrity or transparency. Entrepreneurs must navigate the fine line between leveraging secrets for competitive advantage and engaging in practices that undermine trust or exploit vulnerable populations.

For instance, consider the ethical implications of data collection in startups. Many successful companies have thrived by harnessing consumer data to tailor their offerings. However, this practice raises questions about privacy and consent. Startups must prioritize ethical data practices, ensuring that they respect consumer rights while still capitalizing on valuable insights.

Moreover, there is a responsibility to share knowledge and insights with others in the entrepreneurial ecosystem. While competition is inherent in business, fostering a culture of collaboration can lead to collective growth and innovation. Startups should consider how their discoveries can benefit not only their bottom line but also the broader community.

Cultivating an Environment for Discovery

To unlock the value of secrets, entrepreneurs must cultivate an environment conducive to discovery and creativity. This involves fostering a culture that encourages experimentation, risk-taking, and open dialogue. By creating spaces where team members feel empowered to share ideas and challenge assumptions, startups can tap into collective intelligence and uncover hidden insights.

Leadership plays a crucial role in this process. Founders should model curiosity and openness, demonstrating a willingness to explore unconventional ideas. Regular brainstorming sessions, feedback loops, and cross-functional collaboration can stimulate innovative thinking and help identify undiscovered insights within the organization.

Additionally, investing in continuous learning is vital. Startups should encourage team members to pursue professional development opportunities, attend industry conferences, and engage with thought leaders. This commitment to learning can expose entrepreneurs to new perspectives and trends that may reveal untapped potentials.

Conclusion: Embracing Secrets for Success

The role of secrets—undiscovered insights and untapped potentials—cannot be underestimated in the realm of successful startups. Entrepreneurs who recognize and leverage these elements position themselves for innovation and growth in an ever-evolving marketplace. However, this pursuit must be balanced with ethical considerations and a commitment to integrity.

As startups navigate their journeys, they should embrace curiosity and foster environments that encourage exploration and creativity. By doing so, they not only unlock their own potential but also contribute to a vibrant entrepreneurial ecosystem that thrives on collaboration and shared knowledge.

In conclusion, the secrets that lie beneath the surface of conventional wisdom hold immense value for those willing to seek them out. By embracing these insights and potentials, entrepreneurs can pave their paths to success while making meaningful contributions to society at large. In a world driven by innovation, it is those who dare to uncover the secrets that will ultimately shape the future.

Chapter 9

Long-term Planning

The Advantages of Prioritizing Sustainable Growth Over Immediate Results

In the ever growing world of business, the temptation to prioritize immediate results can be overwhelming. Startups and established companies alike often feel the pressure to deliver quick wins—whether through rapid sales growth, aggressive marketing campaigns, or short-term profitability. However, this focus on immediate outcomes can come at a significant cost. Long-term planning, emphasizing sustainable growth, offers a more strategic approach that not only ensures the longevity of a business but also fosters resilience and adaptability in an ever-changing marketplace.

The Case for Sustainable Growth

Sustainable growth refers to a company's ability to expand its operations and increase revenue while maintaining a balance between economic, social, and environmental factors. This approach contrasts sharply with the pursuit of short-term gains, which can lead to decisions that may yield immediate benefits but jeopardize long-term viability. Here are several compelling advantages of prioritizing sustainable growth:

1. Building a Strong Foundation

Long-term planning allows businesses to build a strong foundation for future success. By focusing on sustainable practices, organizations can develop robust systems, processes, and cultures that support ongoing growth. This foundation includes investing in employee development, fostering innovation, and establishing a solid customer base that values the brand beyond immediate transactions.

For example, companies like Patagonia have built their brands around sustainability and ethical practices. By prioritizing long-term goals over quick profits, they have cultivated a loyal customer base that appreciates their commitment to environmental responsibility, ultimately leading to sustained financial success.

2. Enhanced Brand Reputation

In today's socially conscious market, consumers increasingly prefer brands that demonstrate a commitment to sustainability and ethical practices. Companies that prioritize long-term planning and sustainable growth are more likely to build a positive reputation among consumers, employees, and stakeholders.

A strong brand reputation not only attracts customers but also fosters loyalty and trust. Organizations like Unilever have embraced sustainability as a core component of their business strategy. By committing to sustainable sourcing and reducing their environmental footprint, they have enhanced their brand image and attracted consumers who align with their values.

3. Resilience Against Market Fluctuations

Businesses that focus solely on immediate results may find themselves vulnerable to market fluctuations and economic downturns. In contrast, companies with a long-term perspective are better equipped to navigate challenges and adapt to changing conditions.

By investing in sustainable practices, such as diversifying product offerings or exploring new markets, businesses can mitigate risks associated with economic volatility. For instance, during the COVID-19 pandemic, companies that had previously prioritized sustainability were often more agile in adapting their operations, whether by pivoting to online sales or implementing health-conscious practices.

4. Attracting Investment

Investors are increasingly looking for companies that prioritize long-term growth and sustainability. By demonstrating a commitment to responsible business practices, organizations can attract investment from individuals and funds focused on environmental, social, and governance (ESG) criteria.

Startups that emphasize sustainable growth are more likely to secure funding from venture capitalists and angel investors who recognize the value of long-term viability over short-lived profits. This investment can fuel further innovation and expansion while reinforcing the company's commitment to responsible practices.

5. Employee Engagement and Retention

A focus on long-term planning fosters a positive workplace culture that prioritizes employee well-being and development. When employees see that their organization is committed to sustainable growth, they are more likely to feel engaged and motivated in their roles.

Investing in employee training, promoting work-life balance, and encouraging professional development contribute to higher job satisfaction and retention rates. Companies like Google have built their success on creating an innovative work environment that prioritizes employee well-being—leading to a motivated workforce that drives long-term success.

6. Innovation as a Core Value

Long-term planning encourages a culture of innovation within organizations. When businesses prioritize sustainable growth, they are more likely to invest in research and development, explore new technologies, and seek innovative solutions to address emerging challenges.

For instance, Tesla's commitment to sustainability has driven its innovation in electric vehicles and renewable energy solutions. By focusing on long-term goals rather than short-term profits, Tesla has positioned itself as a leader in the automotive industry while contributing positively to environmental sustainability.

7. Customer Loyalty and Advocacy

Customers are increasingly drawn to brands that align with their values. By prioritizing sustainable growth, organizations can cultivate deeper relationships with their customers based on shared principles. This loyalty translates into repeat business and advocacy—customers who champion brands they believe in can become powerful marketing assets.

Brands like TOMS Shoes have successfully leveraged their commitment to social responsibility by adopting a "one-for-one" model—donating a pair of shoes for every pair sold. This approach not only drives sales but also fosters customer loyalty among socially conscious consumers.

Conclusion: A Strategic Imperative

In conclusion, the advantages of prioritizing sustainable growth over immediate results are manifold. Long-term planning enables businesses to build strong foundations, enhance brand reputations, cultivate resilience against market fluctuations, attract investment, engage employees, foster innovation, and cultivate customer loyalty.

While the allure of quick wins may be tempting, entrepreneurs must recognize that true success lies in adopting a holistic approach that balances immediate outcomes with long-term vision. By embracing sustainable growth as a strategic imperative, organizations can position themselves for enduring success in an increasingly complex and competitive landscape.

Ultimately, the journey toward sustainable growth is not just about financial metrics; it is about creating lasting value for all stakeholders—employees, customers, communities, and the environment. As businesses navigate the complexities of today's marketplace, those who prioritize long-term planning will emerge as leaders in their industries, paving the way for a more sustainable future.

Chapter 10

The Importance of Culture

How a Robust Company Culture Encourages Innovation and Teamwork

In today's competitive business landscape, the significance of company culture cannot be overstated. A robust organizational culture serves as the backbone of an enterprise, influencing everything from employee satisfaction to innovation and teamwork. As companies strive to adapt to rapid changes in technology and consumer preferences, fostering a strong culture becomes essential not only for attracting talent but also for driving sustainable success. This chapter explores the critical role that company culture plays in encouraging innovation and teamwork, providing insights on how organizations can cultivate a culture that empowers their workforce.

Understanding Company Culture

Company culture encompasses the shared values, beliefs, and behaviors that shape how employees interact with each other and approach their work. It includes aspects such as communication styles, decision-making processes, and the overall work environment. A positive culture promotes a sense of belonging and purpose, while a negative culture can lead to disengagement and high turnover rates.

The essence of company culture lies in its ability to create an environment where employees feel valued and motivated. This environment is crucial for fostering innovation—the process of generating new ideas, products, or methods—and teamwork—the collaborative effort of individuals working towards a common goal.

The Link Between Culture and Innovation

1. **Encouraging Creativity**: A robust company culture fosters an atmosphere where creativity can thrive. When employees feel safe to express their ideas without fear of criticism, they are more likely to contribute innovative solutions. Companies like Google exemplify this principle by promoting open communication and providing platforms for idea-sharing, such as hackathons and innovation labs. These initiatives encourage employees to think outside the box and explore new possibilities.

2. **Risk-Taking**: Innovation often involves taking risks. A supportive culture encourages employees to experiment and learn from failures rather than penalizing them for missteps. Organizations that celebrate calculated risk-taking create a mindset where employees are willing to explore unconventional solutions. For instance, Amazon's "failure-friendly" culture allows teams to

pursue bold projects, leading to groundbreaking innovations like Amazon Prime and Alexa.

3. **Cross-Functional Collaboration**: A strong culture breaks down silos between departments, promoting cross-functional collaboration. When employees from different backgrounds and expertise come together, they can combine their diverse perspectives to tackle complex challenges creatively. Companies like Pixar have demonstrated the power of collaborative culture by encouraging teams from various disciplines—animation, storytelling, and technology—to work closely together, resulting in innovative films that resonate with audiences.

The Role of Culture in Teamwork

1. **Building Trust**: Trust is the foundation of effective teamwork. A positive company culture fosters trust among team members by promoting transparency and open communication. When employees feel confident that their colleagues have their best interests at heart, they are more likely to collaborate effectively. Trust-building initiatives, such as team-building exercises and regular feedback sessions, can enhance relationships within teams.

2. **Shared Goals**: A robust culture aligns employees around shared goals and values. When team members understand the organization's mission and vision, they are more likely to work cohesively towards achieving

common objectives. This alignment creates a sense of purpose that drives collaboration and enhances overall team performance.

3. **Recognition and Celebration**: Recognizing individual and team contributions reinforces a culture of teamwork. Celebrating successes—whether big or small—encourages employees to support one another and fosters a sense of camaraderie. Companies like Zappos have built their reputation on recognizing employee achievements, which strengthens team bonds and motivates individuals to contribute their best efforts.

Cultivating a Culture of Innovation and Teamwork

To harness the power of company culture in driving innovation and teamwork, organizations must take intentional steps:

1. **Define Core Values**: Clearly articulate the organization's core values and ensure they are integrated into every aspect of the business—from hiring practices to performance evaluations. Employees should understand how these values translate into everyday behavior.

2. **Empower Employees**: Provide employees with the autonomy to make decisions and take ownership of their work. Empowered employees are more likely to contribute innovative ideas and collaborate effectively with their peers.

3. **Encourage Continuous Learning**: Foster a culture of continuous learning by offering training programs, workshops, and opportunities for professional development. When employees feel supported in their growth, they are more likely to take initiative and explore new ideas.

4. **Facilitate Open Communication**: Create channels for open dialogue where employees can share feedback, ideas, and concerns without fear of retribution. Regular check-ins, town hall meetings, and anonymous suggestion boxes can help facilitate communication.

5. **Lead by Example**: Leadership plays a crucial role in shaping company culture. Leaders must embody the values they wish to instill in their teams by demonstrating transparency, accountability, and a commitment to collaboration.

Conclusion

A robust company culture is not merely a "nice-to-have" but a strategic imperative for organizations seeking to thrive in today's dynamic business environment. By fostering an atmosphere that encourages innovation and teamwork, companies can unlock the full potential of their workforce. As organizations prioritize culture alongside strategy, they will find themselves better equipped to navigate challenges, seize opportunities, and drive sustainable growth.

In summary, investing in a strong company culture yields dividends that extend far beyond employee satisfaction; it cultivates an environment where innovation flourishes and teamwork thrives, ultimately positioning organizations for long-term success in an increasingly competitive marketplace.

Conclusion

Embracing the Journey from Nothing to Something New

As we close the pages of "From Nothing to Something New: Insights On Startups, And Build the Future Through Innovation," it becomes clear that the journey of entrepreneurship is not merely about creating a business; it is about igniting a vision and transforming ideas into tangible realities. Throughout this book, we have explored the essence of innovation, the power of resilience, and the importance of a supportive community in nurturing groundbreaking ideas.

In a world that is constantly evolving, the call for original thinking has never been more urgent. Entrepreneurs and aspiring innovators hold the key to shaping the future—one idea at a time. Each chapter has underscored that success does not stem from perfection but from the courage to take risks, learn from failures, and adapt to changing circumstances. The stories of startups that began as mere concepts serve as a testament to what is possible when passion meets perseverance.

As you reflect on your own journey—whether you are an entrepreneur, an aspiring business owner, or an investor—consider the impact you can make by pursuing originality. The marketplace is saturated with imitation; however, true innovation emerges when you dare to think differently. Seek out those unique ideas that resonate with your values and vision. Embrace the challenges that come with building something new, for they are often the catalysts for growth and discovery.

Investors too play a pivotal role in this ecosystem. Your support can help turn visionary ideas into reality. By backing original concepts and fostering innovative startups, you contribute not only to individual success stories but also to a broader culture of creativity and progress. Your investment can empower entrepreneurs to challenge the status quo and bring forth solutions that address pressing global issues.

As we look ahead, let us remember that every great advancement begins with a single thought—a spark of inspiration that has the potential to change lives. Whether you are developing a product, launching a service, or investing in a groundbreaking idea, commit to pursuing originality with unwavering determination. The future is not something we inherit; it is something we create together.

So, I urge you, take action. Move deep into your passions, explore uncharted territories, and collaborate with others who share your vision. Surround yourself with a network of like-minded individuals who inspire and challenge you. Share your ideas openly, seek feedback, and be willing to pivot when necessary.

In conclusion, let us embark on this journey of innovation with open hearts and minds. Together, we can transform nothing into something new—contributing to a future rich with possibilities and advancements that elevate humanity. The world is waiting for your unique contributions; don't hold back. Chase those original ideas and become a catalyst for change. The future is yours to build—let's innovate it together!

References

- World Economic Forum. (2021). *The Future of Jobs Report 2021*. Retrieved from [WEF](https://www.weforum.org/reports/the-future-of-jobs-report-2021)
- Tesla Inc. (n.d.). *Sustainable Energy Products*. Retrieved from [Tesla](https://www.tesla.com/sustainability)
- Impossible Foods. (n.d.). *Our Mission*. Retrieved from [Impossible Foods](https://impossiblefoods.com/our-mission/)